AM ASSOCIATES:
Complete Guide:

Make Money Online with Amazon Associates

The Amazon Associates Bible: A Step-By-Step Guide on Amazon Associates Affiliate Program

By Dan Johnson

Published by Media Prestige eBook Publishing Company

© Copyright 2014

Table of Contents

INTRODUCTION

Hi, Friend! Thank you for purchasing this book. I have written this book to share with you a complete guide on Amazon Associates affiliate program and how you can make money online through this affiliate system.

By reading this, you will gain more information on how to make niche websites and have a steady income for the rest of your life.

In this book, I will guide you through the step-by-step process on how to start an online business that will help you generate an income through Amazon's affiliate program. I will also discuss in the simplest way what affiliate marketing is and why among all others, Amazon's program is the better option for you when you start an online business.

I'll show you how to choose the right niche market, and also the advantages and options of having your own website.

This is a simple yet very informative guide on how to be an Amazon Affiliate.

In fact, I wrote this book not requiring you to be internet savvy. I'm sure that you can do each step in this book even if you're a beginner. I have also added several illustrations and short video tutorials to help you visualize the tasks being discussed. I encourage you to watch the video links especially if you haven't created a blog or a website yet.

When I had my first blog, I got so excited, and I'm sure you'll feel the same. You will learn how to get started with Amazon Associates and promote top selling products on your website.

This book will also give you the best secret tips that successful Amazon affiliates do, so you can follow them and maximize your earnings as an Affiliate. I also listed the best practices on how to avoid being banned in Amazon.

If you're already an Amazon Affiliate and have your own niche website, you can proceed to **Chapter 5: Start Promoting Products** of this book.

So, what more can you ask for? Establishing your own online business is right at your fingertips and you'll be on your road to making money online with Amazon affiliate program!

I can guarantee that if you follow all the steps in this book, you can have a good start on your online business.

I encourage you to read this book from start to finish and don't let anything stop you from pursuing what you've started. You might get hesitated and confused but keep on learning until you live the life you want to have.

I'm here to guide you, so are you ready now? You're about to read your one great decision to make money online.

So relax, grab your favorite snacks while learning these new concepts. After all, it's fun to learn and make money!

And now, let's begin!

CHAPTER 1: WHAT IS AMAZON AFFILIATE MARKETING?

Amazon affiliate marketing program has been offering a money making opportunity online since 1996. Considerably, it is one of the first online affiliate marketing programs that introduced a simple and convenient way to earn passive income as an affiliate marketer. It has been on the web for almost 18 years and you might be wondering why many bloggers still opt to make it as an Amazon Affiliate. But, before going any further into Amazon affiliate program, I'd like to discuss a short background of affiliate marketing.

Affiliate marketing isn't a new business model in the internet world, right? I think you have encountered various affiliate marketing programs as well.

Affiliate marketing programs provide an online income stream for ordinary people who want to earn money online, which is considered to be a popular online business nowadays.

Yes, affiliate marketing is a good way to start making money online.

In simple terms, we can define Affiliate marketing as something that allows internet marketers to get rewards for promoting other people's products with an agreed commission. And the common venue is through the affiliate marketer's blog or website. In most affiliate marketing programs, an affiliate marketer earns from a link on its blog that refers the visitors to another network and create a purchase.

Unfortunately, it is not an overnight scheme to make money online, but affiliate marketing can be a decent way to profit if you're serious about making it a business. Perhaps, affiliate marketing is better than other advertising networks like Google Adsense and Ad Networks to make money from blogs, because ads displayed on blogs may bring uncomfortable feeling to the reader.

Nonetheless, an affiliate marketer needs to learn from a step-by-step guide to come up with the best strategies to make it profitable.

Since you're geared towards building a business as an affiliate marketer, there are critical decisions involved to come up with favorable results. One of which is to choose the affiliate network and products that you can incorporate into your website. I find it advantageous for you to get started with one of the oldest and most trusted affiliate marketing programs, and that is through the Amazon affiliate marketing program called **Amazon Associates**.

Amazon Associates page: https://goo.gl/bMBy7C

a. Why Should You Choose Amazon?

Here are some reasons why Amazon affiliate marketing program is the preferable program to start making money online:

1. Sells a wide range of reputable products

There is a variety of products to promote as soon as you've set up a website. This gives a venue to get more quality and relevant products for recommendations or reviews on your site. You can be selective and recommend only the products which you have tried or you truly believe in.

2. Millions of people are buying every day.

People trust Amazon, so there is a great chance that your readers won't think twice to purchase when they click your affiliate link to Amazon. And most likely, readers who will visit your website have already an Amazon account.

3. Straightforward and dependable payments.

You control how you want to receive your commissions, without requiring any irrelevant conditions to be met before Amazon issue the payments.

4. Income raises as you sell more items.

The percentage commission increases when more products are sold in a given month. Thus, it gives you an opportunity to have higher rates when more products are sold from your referred links.

5. Site-wide coverage of Cookies.

Amazon gives you a site-wide coverage of cookies*. This means you can still earn from any product that a referred visitor buys, even if it's not the product that is linked from your website. On the other hand, other affiliates find it disadvantageous to only have a 24-hour cookie window on their website.

* Cookies are primarily used to store login information for a specific site and to identify web users. Most of the e-commerce sites are using session cookies to store items placed in shopping cart.

Definitely, I can say that Amazon Associates is a perfect affiliate marketing program for you to earn online. Here is an illustration that will show you how affiliate marketing works with your own website and Amazon.

One of the most important details you need to know about the Amazon affiliate program is how you can earn from this. Well, there is no such thing as a guaranteed amount of earning in any online business. It only depends on how much work you exert to maximize the benefits of affiliate marketing like the Amazon.

But, would you not consider an average of 4% to 10% commission as a really good start for you, just by recommending several products on your website?

I will show you how Amazon rewards their affiliates by having affiliate links on websites.

Basically, as an Amazon affiliate, your contributions to their business are rewarded by unit volume and growth. What does this mean? In joining Amazon Associates, you are allowed to earn higher fees by generating an adequate volume of sales through links on your website. This volume of sales comes from "special links" that your referrals click on from your site and lead them to purchase a product.

Your earning will start from 4% commission rate, even with only 1 general product sold, and can reach up to 8.5% with more than 3,130 products sold in any given month. The 4% to 8.5% commission rate is a volume-based advertising fee rates from Amazon, where rates are increased as the number of products sold to increase.

The table below shows how Amazon will reward you based on the number of products purchased by your referrals as they clicked a "special link" on your website.

Number of Products Shipped/Downloaded in a Given Month**	Volume-Based Advertising Fee Rates for General Products
1–6	4.00%
7–30	6.00%
31–110	6.50%
111–320	7.00%
321–630	7.50%
631–1570	8.00%
1571–3130	8.25%
3131+	8.50%

As I have mentioned, Amazon has a wide range of products. You can still earn from products with fixed advertising fee rates, which ranges from 1% to 10% aside from the volume-based advertising fee rates for general products shown above. You can choose from the product categories below to review and recommend on your website.

Product Category	Fixed Advertising Fee Rates
Electronics Products	4.00%
Amazon MP3 Products	5.00%
Amazon Instant Video Products	5.00%
Game Downloads Products	6.00%
Gift Cards Redeemable on amazon.com	6.00%
Gift Cards Not Redeemable on amazon.com	4.00%
Magazine Products	6.00%

Grocery Products (including Prime Pantry)	4.00%
Video Game Console Products	1.00%
Headphones Products	6.00%
DVD Products	4.00%
Jewelry Products	6.00%
Industrial Products	6.00%
Products available on any site other than www.amazon.com	0.00%

With these schemes, another essential action is to choose products with good advertising fee rates while considering your website niche and the interest of your readers. This ensures a potential income. It is also important that you are familiar with the Amazon qualifying lists of products when you make an affiliate link on your website. Don't worry; you'll learn more about this as you read the other chapters.

b. Amazon Payment Methods

As an Amazon affiliate, this is the information you've been waiting for.

Here's the deal!

You'll get paid by Amazon on a monthly basis for qualifying purchases of your referrals. They'll be sending you the earning approximately 60 days after the end of each month. You have to make sure that you've selected your preferred payment method.

Here are the payment methods you can choose from:

1. Direct Deposit Payment.

Choosing this payment method requires you to designate a valid bank account where Amazon will deposit your earning. With this payment method, your earning must be at least $10 for Amazon to deposit it.

2. Amazon.com Gift Card.

You will receive your earnings in a form of a gift card from Amazon with your earning's exact amount. This gift card is redeemable for products on Amazon.com. They can also withhold your earning if you have not yet reached at least $10 commission.

3. Check Payment.

This payment method requires you to have an earning of at least $100 commission before Amazon can pay you by check. Also, there will be a $15 deduction for the processing fee of every check they will send you.

Amazon's payment method option is another advantage of Amazon Associates. Some of the affiliates find it appropriate to be paid for products by using a gift card instead of cash. Other affiliates sometimes use the gift card as token or prize to their loyal followers.

On the other hand, payment by check is not usually preferred by affiliates. Although, some affiliates consider it as an investment, which commission matures over time by just adding links to Amazon on a regular basis and wait until successful referral comes.

For affiliates, the earning below $10 is a fair amount to withhold payment. Given that, I think it is a far less amount compared to other affiliate marketing programs.

There are tons to learn in affiliate marketing, and you might be overwhelmed with it. And so, I encourage you to take it slow. It takes time to learn, be able to apply strategies in affiliate marketing, and be successful. You are assured that all the hard work will be worth it as long as you're doing the right process.

This is the perfect time for you to get going and pursue your online business with your own website. Not all may succeed in affiliate marketing, but there can be a significant earning each month with Amazon Associate if you practice proven strategies of affiliate marketers, which I'll share on this book.

Don't be lured with common misconceptions of getting rich quick schemes, particularly in the internet world. This chapter will reveal a money making opportunity, which is the #1 way to make passive income online, and not a get rich quick scheme.

This is my short introduction to Amazon Associates and affiliate marketing. I'm certain that it will help you understand the online business you're about to launch.

On the next chapters, I will be giving you a detailed step-by-step guide on how to start your online business from ground zero as promised. Focus as you read on. Enjoy your reading with your snack and a glass of drink, if you want.

CHAPTER 2: FIND A NICHE

Getting started with your online business begins with a question, "What kinds of products should I promote?" To answer this question, you need to do a niche market research. In this chapter, I will discuss niche market research that will help you to develop the overall topic your niche website.

First, let me define what a niche market is.

A niche market is defined as a small market segment that is determined to have a profit potential for a business.

Finding the right and hot niche market is an essential part of building your income as an affiliate. Getting the right niche generates traffic to your website and eventually generates more income for you; otherwise, if you get the wrong one, your website may exist without the possibility to pull traffic, or may get traffic but won't generate successful revenue for you.

Most online businesses are targeting specific niche markets as compared to having broad markets. Specific niche makes a better foundation to have a progressive online business. You have to do some research and explore a topic so you'll have an idea on the market you wish to pursue. And so, you have to make this step as interesting as possible. Niche research may take time and needs mental focus but getting the appropriate result is rewarding.

In finding your niche, you may think of your expertise or interest. Familiarity with your niche will be in your favor when you begin creating your website content and promoting your products. You can do this by assessing your educational and career background, as well as your family's business, if any, as the basis of your niche. Then, start your research on it.

You're not supposed to build a website based only on your instincts. When you have an idea on the niche you want to pursue, it should be accompanied with data. Definitely, you need to do niche research, and that involves keyword research as well.

I'm strongly pointing out that a niche research will benefit an aspiring affiliate marketer when it is done from the start of the online business. On this chapter, I will guide you through the initial step to make money online with Amazon.

a. How to Find a Profitable Niche?

Finding a niche may take a long process. Here a list that will help you speed up the process and decide on your niche:

1. Get specific market with specific needs.

The word "specific" is the main thought here. From a bigger idea, you must think of possible subcategories until you find the most specific need and market that you want to promote with Amazon affiliate links.

For example, you're interested in addressing the need of people who want to lose weight. It will definitely give you a number of search engine results. But, it isn't beneficial when you stick to a broad market such as losing weight.

To be specific, you need to identify which means of losing weight your niche will be; is it by exercise, diet, supplements, or pills?

More so, find the specific market with its subsets such as the gender, age group, and even capacity to purchase that you like to target. Once you have the idea, start your research to get a more specific topic.

2. Find niche keywords if there is sufficient market for your selected niche.

One of the best tools used to find the search volumes for a niche keyword is **Keyword Tool API** . With this tool, you'll be able to get 750 Google keyword suggestions for free. This ensures that your website contains content that is created around the right keywords. It auto-suggests keywords that your potential customers are already using to search for products.

Keyword Tool website: http://keywordtool.io/

Do this by selecting either a phrase or exact match when finding keywords. It helps if you use long tail keywords with a minimum of 3 words in checking SEO competition. Though long tail keywords may result in fewer search volumes, it can show less competition for that particular niche. And that may be advantageous also for you because your website will have greater chance to drive traffic in a lesser competition.

On the other hand, having the very specific keywords will show immediate results of what your targeted readers want.

The result will show you how sufficient the market is and if you'll be willing to compete with the top SEO performers of your chosen niche.

Consequently, your niche keywords that have the highest search results can be your domain name when you start building your website.

3. Determine the real SEO competition of your niche.

The niche research you'll do tackles more about SEO. The truth is in online business, there is a high competition especially when you have chosen the best niche markets on the internet. This is the part of finding a niche which requires your full attention because, honestly, SEO is not easy.

There are harder and competitive niches in affiliate marketing, but still more opportunities remain to be tapped though may be difficult. Regardless which type of niche you choose, you need to set your time, expectations and expertise with your highest ability in finding and promoting your niche.

The best way in determining the SEO competition of your niche is to check the Top 10 results of the keywords you selected. This means that your targeted keywords are actually ranking on top.

b. Key Factors in Selecting a Niche

The process of finding a niche involves several factors. In deciding your niche market, you must be able to consider the following:

1. **Huge demand** of the niche
2. **Long-standing** capacity of the niche
3. **Capability to compete** with other competitors
4. **Availability of products** (physical or digital)
5. **Promoting a passion**

Let me point out each factor to help you find a good niche while you do niche research.

1. Huge demand of the niche

A huge demand of the niche can be checked through keyword research as mentioned above or you can take advantage of your Facebook account to do some test advertisement and check the response from your targeted market. Definitely, if there is a positive response to it, your chosen niche is a topic you can pursue.

2. Long-standing capacity of the niche

When finding a niche, consider if it can stay for a long period of time. It may be ideal to choose a niche that you know will be sought for in the next 5-10 years.

The best niches are those that are timeless. It's best to build your website with a long-standing niche as compared to a seasonal one.

3. Capability to compete with other competitors

As you check the Top 10 results of your keyword research, check if you can actually compete with them. The fact that a niche has a high competition means there's a lot of money on it, you just need to determine your tolerance level of competition and how long you can commit to that niche.

4. Availability of products (physical or digital)

Amazon offers a wide range of products, but you have to be sure that your target niche has the products available on Amazon. Generally speaking, most online users are interested in having a physical and digital product. Find a niche that can offer both a physical and digital item which you can promote on your website to maximize opportunities in affiliate marketing.

5. Promoting a passion

Personally speaking, it's hard to do a task that doesn't interest me. I may be able to do it but it will take time to really come up what I expect it to be. It can be tiresome at some point, isn't it? But, even if you are not interested in a certain niche, you can at least be passionate about what you do.

And in this case, your passion for doing affiliate marketing through your website should tantamount to your passion for a potentially profitable niche whether the niche doesn't interest you much. It could be your passion to help other people with their needs that can serve as an inspiration for you to passionately write about that niche.

Again, this step needs your focus and time to research. Don't be discouraged because there are tools available to help you in select the right niche.

The **Google Keyword Planner** is a tool you can use to search what customers are looking for. You can search for keywords and ad group ideas to see how it might perform. Also, you get historical statistics and traffic forecasts with this tool. This tool will help you not only in the beginning of your online business but all throughout your website campaigns.

Google Keyword Planner: http://goo.gl/kP7mWf

To give you an idea on how to do use keyword tools, watch the following YouTube tutorials. Just click on the title to open the link.

- **New Free Keyword Tool:** https://goo.gl/HhyYbv
- **How to do proper keyword research and find buyers keywords with the Google Keyword Planner**: https://goo.gl/YQ5387

Think of it this way: you are finding a niche that you think online users are interested on and possibly willing to spend money when they read your product review. Most importantly, your niche must fulfill the needs of your website visitors as well as yours.

Are you already thinking of possible niches you're interested in working on? List all the ideas you have in mind. Keep it for a while and read the next chapter about building your website.

CHAPTER 3: BUILD A WEBSITE

Why is building your own website is a good idea for affiliate marketing?

There are many internet marketers who take advantage of social networking sites like Facebook and Google to do their online business. You may make money on it without a website, but when you build your own online business, you must build a website that you can call your own. Website owners are said to have a virtual real estate that becomes their property and gets higher value over time.

You have control over your own website unlike with social networking sites. What if after building a Facebook page and made lots of income from it, then Facebook had some modifications and decided to remove your page. What would you do then? Are you willing to start all over again?

Creating your own customer base requires you to build your own website to ensure continuity and longevity of your online business as an Affiliate Marketer.

a. How to Choose your Website Niche Topic?

This chapter will guide you on how you can build your own website or blog as the venue for your Amazon affiliate links. If you already have your own blog, keep browsing this chapter for other tips; there might be some information that you haven't applied yet when you built your website.

Let me share the first few tasks to do in setting up your own website.

1. Know what interests you.

Once you have selected a niche, I suppose that you have selected the one that interests you.
Remember, you should build a website that will reflect yourself, your passion, and ideas you want to share with other people.

It is a niche that you will not get bored when you start updating your website. Also, you'll be reviewing and recommending products to your visitors, so you better have a topic that fits your knowledge and taste.

2. Choose a narrower topic.

It is preferable to have a specific topic that addresses a particular market, and so choosing a narrower topic for your website is advisable. You can also set up categories to maintain organized posts, and just make sure to be focused on your topic. The niche research you learned in the previous chapter will guide you to choose a narrower topic.

3. Research on your chosen topic.

With your research, you'll have a clearer goal for your target audience and you can be specific on products you may wish to review and recommend on your website. You may also visit Amazon.com for more ideas; after all, you'll be marketing their products.

4. Have your main keyword in your URL or domain name.

When you've decided your most preferred topic, you have to choose a better keyword for your URL or domain name. Your website name will tell more about the topic of your blog.

Your URL should be close to what online users usually typed on the search engine box when they search about their interests. If you plan to have weight loss as your niche, then a URL of www.weightloss.com is better than www.johnsmithblog.com. This will help you a great deal when it comes to your page ranking in Google when people search for your keyword.

5. Know some basic formatting.

You have to get accustomed with inserting images, hyperlinks, and some basic text formatting. These are basic website features you need to learn, especially in designing your website to have a more professional look. Though most of the website building platforms are easy to use, you'll get to understand basic functions of different codes as you go along.

6. Think of a theme.

Think of a perfect theme that reflects your website's purpose. Your theme should capture the interest of your visitors. You have to make them feel comfortable and happy when they visit your website. This is one way to get the attention of visitors and eventually gain avid viewers of your blog.

At an early stage, you just need to have an idea of the theme you want for your website so that you won't take much time in selecting a theme when you start creating your website.

You don't need to worry much about your theme because one of the best features of website building platforms, particularly WordPress, is the variety of templates available for users. You can choose from different themes without designing it on your own.

b. Kinds of Web Hosting Services

Once you're done with the first few tasks, you can now start choosing your website building platform.

Here are 2 hosting services to choose from so you can start building your website:

Option 1: Free hosting website

There are website building platforms like **Blogger**, **Weebly** and **WordPress** where you can create your blog for free with basic features. This is the least option, if you don't have a budget yet to buy a hosted website. Though the website is free, once you use it to earn money, there are some platforms that get their own cut from what you are earning from your blog, and that could be a 50% cut.

Blogger: http://www.blogger.com/
Weebly: https://www.weebly.com/start/blog
WordPress: http://www.wordpress.com/create/

Don't start your blog in these free platforms if you decide to buy your own domain in the future. If you have an article at **www.weightloss.wordpress.com/example** that's number one in Google search and decide to migrate your website to a private domain, your link to that article will change to **www.weightloss.com/example**.

So, to sum it up, if you plan to buy your own domain in the future, don't start investing your time and effort in a free platform.

Among many website building platforms, most of the bloggers prefer WordPress as their platform because of the following reasons:

- It has many different lay outs and free themes

- It's easy to write blog posts, add pictures and images

- It has a feature for comment and share

- Posts can be categorized

With a free website, you can only have a sub-domain, for example, *yourwebsitename.wordpress.com,* though it is a bit awkward for some who use it for online business because it doesn't have a professional look.

Here are the steps to build a free blog with WordPress:

Step #1: Sign up an account

Go to *www.wordpress.com*. This will only take a few minutes and you can start your free website. You'll need your email address, preferred URL or name, username, and password. Then, fill out all needed details.

Step #2: Check your email

Once you're done with all the details, check your email for the final step of registration and click the link from the email to activate your account. Make sure to activate your account within 2 days.

Step #3: Log in to Wordpress.com

Go to *www.wordpress.com* and your website is now activated and ready to use. Go to your dashboard to start setting up your website.

Step #4: Design your website

In the dashboard, check the application management menus to set up your blog. You can choose from the 'Free Themes' library which one suits your preference and the niche you've chosen.

You can see *Settings>General Settings* in the dashboard where you will be required to type in the name and tagline for your blog. The name you will enter appears in the header which your readers will see when they view your website.

You may need to add widgets in *Appearance>Widgets* to enhance the design and functionality of your blog. The most common widgets are Categories, Archives, an Email subscription and a Facebook Like box. Decide on different widgets which you may want to add on to your website and rearrange them in a more presentable layout.

I have listed here video tutorials to help you create your free website. Click on the title to link you on YouTube tutorials:

YouTube Tutorials:
- **How to Sign up For Wordpress.com Blog for Business:** https://goo.gl/4XNQB7
- **WordPress Dashboard Overview:** https://goo.gl/uZXdTh
- **Using WordPress Themes:** https://goo.gl/DTET5k

Though it won't cost you a penny to have your website with free hosting, you may find it disadvantageous to have some advertisements run on your website by WordPress. If you don't want them to place ads on your website, you need to pay almost $30 a year. This is one reason why other bloggers prefer a premium account.

Also, there are some restrictions in customizing your website with a free one as compared from having a premium account where you can have more options to customize your website.

One important thing to note, if you will sign up at *www.wordpress.com*, you have to make sure that you're aware of its Terms of Service because if you happen to violate it, they can delete your website anytime. More so, the free service provider has all the rights to remove your website anytime they choose.

Option 2: Paid hosting website

There are two types of paid hosting website, the website built from an upgraded version with a premium plan and a website built with a self-hosting service provider.

1. Premium Plan website builder

For beginners who can allot some budget to build a website, a premium or business plan is available to website building platforms such as Wordpress.

Same steps as the free platform will be done to build a website, but you'll be paying around $99 to $299 per year for a Premium and Business Plan respectively and get advanced customization of your website. And so, it gives you more control to customize your website. These plans actually look more professional especially that you can have a custom *.com, .net, .org, .co, .me* website address to choose from.

Here is the list of WordPress upgraded features aside from its Blog feature:

- Custom design

- VideoPress

- Direct Email or Chat Support

- Greater GB for storage

This can be a good option for a beginner because you won't need to code a website from scratch. The plans are incorporated with tools and features in an easy-to-use platform. If you're not quite decided yet to take the Premium or Business Plan, you may opt to take a free trial for 14 days.

Different themes are available from these plans, but if you require having custom themes or plugins on your website, you can do it with a self-hosted WordPress.

2. Self-hosting service provider

Internet marketers who aim to make it big in affiliate marketing prefer to build a self-hosted website. This allows the website owner to get full control of the blog as compared to free platforms or premium plans. Self-hosting is providing a server that connects remotely your blog to the internet.

This type of website is what you usually see when you search on the internet with URL name like *www.websitename.com*. Website owners have their own domain which approximately costs $7 to $13 a year and a self-hosting server which costs from $4 to $8 a month. This sums up a cost of around $55 to $109 a year if you decide to take this option to build your website.

When you opt to buy your own domain and pay for a self-hosting server, you can cancel it anytime if you find it not suited for you. You may also prefer services which offer a 90-day money back guarantee.

Most bloggers prefer getting a domain and hosting from the same source to save money and time. One important matter to consider is to have a website builder that offers customer support service to professionally attend all inquiries and concerns in maintaining the website.

You won't have a difficult time choosing a hosting service provider for your website. Just make sure it has WordPress plugins, though most providers do have it. Most website owners take advantage of installing WordPress plugins because it is an add-on feature that makes the website good for visitors.

Here is a guide to building your self-hosted website:

Step #1: Get a Domain Name

This is the URL keyword that you've decided and you prefer to name your website. You'll be paying your domain name annually to have the right to use it.

It is like getting a name of a business, though any individual can register a domain name without necessarily creating a company.

Why is a domain name important to your online business?
A simple answer is that it gives more credibility to you because most people are willing to do business with a website that has a domain name.

It is an easy process. Domain name registration is an assurance of your ownership.

A domain registrar is like a big bank of all titles of website ownership or domains. Thus, they make sure of the only owner who can access to the keys to that domain.

You may register your domain name directly with a domain registrar or through a web host. It is preferable to directly register it instead of getting it done through a web host. This is to ensure that you're actually the registered owner of such domain name.

You need to prepare a credit card or **Paypal** account to pay for your domain to allow you to register and claim the domain name immediately. Few of the most popular domain name registrars are **GoDaddy, Namecheap, 1&1 Internet**, and **Dotster**. Upon registering, you become responsible for protecting your domain registration login.

- **PayPal:** http://www.paypal.com/
- **GoDaddy:** http://www.godaddy.com/
- **Namecheap:** http://www.namecheap.com/
- **1&1 Internet:** http://www.1and1.com/
- **Dotster:** http://www.dotster.com/

Step #2: Set up a web host

You'll need web hosting to provide you with space on the internet for your website. It's a gateway to publish your contents with a web hosting service.

There are many web hosts available on the internet, and most of it meets the minimum requirements of WordPress to make it work at its best. If you're looking for a web host, most website users prefer **Bluehost, DreamHost, GoDaddy** or **HostGator.** It's important that your web host has PHP and MySQL and a cPanel for easy WordPress installation. Again, you'll be paying a web host that costs around $4 to $8 a month.

Your web host will provide you unlimited disk storage and monthly data transfer. It also provides webmail addresses and easy install WordPress plugins.

- **Bluehost:** http://www.bluehost.com/
- **DreamHost:** http://www.dreamhost.com/
- **GoDaddy:** http://www.godaddy.com/
- **HostGator:** http://www.hostgator.com/

Step #3: Install WordPress from a web host

Once you've signed up with a web host, you're allowed to navigate on the cPanel where it has an auto-installer for WordPress.

Somehow, this platform doesn't need you to be technical. You have a choice to have a website designer to spare you from doing it, but it may cost you more.

Step #4: Log in to WordPress

After you installed WordPress on your web host, log in to your newly installed WordPress account to configure the settings.

Here is a video tutorial to help you install your blog on your paid web host.

YouTube Tutorial:
- **How to Create and Host a Website with WordPress:** https://goo.gl/xDPrMa

Now, you're ready to design your website through WordPress platform. Browse your dashboard when you logged in to set up and design your website.

With a self-hosted website, you can have backups and install custom themes. This makes a self-hosted website different from other options.

Also, it requires own maintenance of the website which you can work on it under your control.

A self-hosted website gives you the full rights on your website, which is the reason why you're paying for it.

In summary, this will illustrate to you the process of building your website:

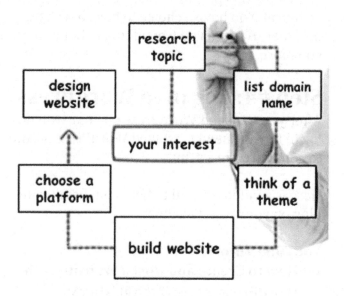

Choose the appropriate platform to build your website. I discussed pertinent information of each option to help you decide on it. You're on your way to having your own website with the straightforward ideas I shared with you.

Let me go further by sharing with you some strategies that will help build up your website, and that is through creating social media networks.

Setting up accounts on social media networks can be beneficial to your website and your online business. It's a way to keep in touch with your readers while having more venues to share your post with affiliate links. It will also improve your search engine ranking (more tips will be given on building traffic in the next chapters).

As part of building your website, you have to develop connections and networks to establish successful marketing strategies.

Setting up social media accounts for your website will benefit you because it:

- Creates more links to your own website

- Generates free and targeted traffic

- Can easily find large volume of users to offer promoted products

Most of the social media networks dedicated to the website are Facebook page, Twitter, Google+ and Pinterest. Here are the advantages of each social media network you can consider to set up:

- **Facebook** - Because of its millions of users, you can find people that belong to your niche market. Shared links with followers can generate traffic.

- **Twitter** - Helps online business share or tweet quality and relevant contents.

- **Google+** - Helps you create a group or circle where people can follow, and also a venue for you to follow others and let people know about your website.

- **Pinterest** - Can generate more traffic by sharing images from your site. A blog post with an image using the keyword of your post can be linked to your Pinterest account.

Designing your social media accounts will be easier because you already have a theme for your website. Your social media account exhibits your website, but not necessarily mirrors it.

To start with your social media network, sign up an account with the same email address you used in setting up your website. Then, another important thing to do is adding the social media buttons. You can do this in two ways:

1. Links from your website directly to your social media accounts.

These are direct links shown either on top or sidebar of your website.

When your website visitors click on the buttons, they will be directed to your social media accounts. It should build your good reputation and communication to encourage readers to patronize your recommended products.

Again, make sure that posts in your social media accounts are not the same content as seen on your website. It could be additional information on what your website is offering.

2. Buttons for social sharing.

These social sharing icons are shown to your visitors that allow them to share your contents to their social media accounts. In this way, more people will get to know more of your blog and get connected with you.

It would be a lot of work if you'll manage many social media accounts for your website. I suggest that you choose your favorite venue so you can concentrate on one social media account.

You may be interested in automating some social sharing with plugins and software. WordPress has a plugin you can set up to share your old posts on Twitter and Facebook. There are also other free or paid dashboards like HootSuite Pro that allows you to control, schedule, and interact more through social media.

Check this YouTube video tutorial about **Tweet Old Post WordPress Plugin** to decide if Twitter can be one of your preferred social media accounts.

Tweet Old Post WordPress Plugin:
https://goo.gl/3BCF9C

Obviously, websites you see on the internet are tied to different social media accounts that have been a proven strategy to get more visitors.

One piece of advice I can give is to never resort to buying likes and followers from your social media network because it will eventually put down your reputation. Just build your network by getting real people and targeted followers.

To end this chapter, building your website is like building a house. You have to keep a well-designed platform that can invite more visitors.

The key is to have a website with good content and more interactive social media account that attract the right followers. The quality of the content matters most than its quantity because it is through your content that Amazon special links will be incorporated.

I encourage you to think very well about all the options I shared in this chapter. Imagine how you would like to see your website few years from now, then, you'll be able to decide on how you'll build your website.

CHAPTER 4: SIGN UP WITH AMAZON ASSOCIATES

Great job! Your journey to your online business is getting more exciting with your own website. But don't worry if you haven't figured it out yet. It normally takes some time to find a niche and build a website.

Just be ready now to start your Amazon Associate affiliate marketing program.

Generally, selection of products you wish to promote should be clear before signing up with Amazon.

It is a crucial step in affiliate marketing, though Amazon offers a wide array of products which can be your basis of selection. It requires some research to ensure that the products on your mind have good standing in the market.

a. How to Select Best Amazon Products to Promote?

To help you build a solid product line which you'll be marketing from Amazon, take note of the following factors to be considered.

1. Target Audience

It will determine who or what group you'd like to visit your website. Get some information on basic demographics and behavior of your target audience. Research on price sensitivity to get an idea of what your target audience is willing to pay for your products.

2. Pricing

When you consider the percentage commission you will be getting from Amazon, the price of your products needs to be reasonably high if you want to get a decent commission for each sale.

For example, a good price tag of at least $200 can give you a good result for your product review and recommendation.

Though, this isn't a primary option. You'll have to consider other factors as well.

3. Demand

Your product must be one of the top searched products or considered to be bestseller products on Amazon. Try to Google a product and check how many results you can get to see if there's enough demand for the product. A good number of search in Google means a product has a potential to be sold.

This still depends on your capability to compete with top searched products.

4. Website Design

Your products need to be reflected on the design of your website. The theme you have chosen will speak for the products you're promoting.

b. How to Build a Product List

At this point, you should be focusing on your product line ideas to clearly identify your niche before you sign up with Amazon Associates. Gather some ideas to find a good niche that is aligned with your chosen topic as you build your website.

Here is a simple guide to find product list with Amazon:

Step #1: Look for the lists

Go to **http://www.amazon.com/gp/bestsellers** to access the easiest resource of looking for product list ideas. This page will show you not only the bestseller list but you can also access other lists such as the top rated, most gifted, most wished for, and hot new products.

The wide array of products on Amazon is enclosed in these sites where you can have many ideas of potentially profitable niches.

Step #2: Pick and sort the details

You may be overwhelmed with Amazon's product list, so it is better that you pick a category, and you may want also to go through the sub-categories. Sorting of the list will give you a better look on the page, whether by relevance, popularity, price or customer review.

From here, you'll have some product ideas that correlate to your website. You may want to watch a video tutorial on how to find a niche on Amazon through the link below.

YouTube tutorial:
- **Find Niche Category Ideas Using Amazon Best Sellers List:** https://goo.gl/eKVWY4

c. How to Join Amazon Associates

When you have a list of product ideas, proceed to join Amazon affiliate program.

Here are the steps in joining the Amazon Associates:

> **Step #1:** Go to **www.affiliate-program.amazon.com** and you will see the main page of Amazon Associate. Click the **"Join Now for Free"** button to start signing up.
>
> Then, select "New Customer" to enter your name and email address. You will be asked to choose a password for your account.
>
> **Step #2:** You will be directed to fill out your account information. This will be their basis as to whom Amazon will issue payment.
>
> **Step #3:** The page will ask you to fill out your website profile. You will give the URL of your domain name, e.g. *http://www.yourwebsitename.com.* Refer to your interest and topic of your website to write a summary about it and select from the list which category does your website belong. Indicate which product line does your website offers.

Step #4: Read the Amazon Associates Operating Agreement and then click" Submit". Feel free to contact Amazon if you have any questions about the application.

Step #5: Check your email for notification from Amazon. This will inform you if your account has been approved. It may take more than 24 hours to get a notification.

Step #6: Start your first affiliate products to your website once your account is approved.

It may take you less than 20 minutes to do Step 1 to 4. Here is a short video tutorial to help you prepare in signing up with Amazon.

YouTube Tutorial:
- **Amazon Affiliate Sign up Step by Step Tutorial:** https://goo.gl/kVaEva

Signing up is easy and it's definitely free to join!

Always be reminded that being an affiliate requires a concrete website niche. It serves as the foundation that attracts the right audience to get results of a profitable income stream with your online business.

The time devoted in identifying your niche is very critical, but as soon as you have decided on it, you'll be 100% ready to work with Amazon Associate.

Try to search the first 2 products you're interested to promote for the launch of your website. Soon, you'll get familiar with the selection of products as you become accustomed to your niche.

Okay, you've selected some products and you probably wonder how to promote the Amazon products on your website.

And so, this is the best time to read the next chapter about promoting products, which is the core of your online business as an affiliate.

CHAPTER 5: START PROMOTING PRODUCTS

I believe by now you understand that affiliate marketing is all about promoting a product. Thus, earning from it depends on how you properly promote products on your website.

Certainly, it requires efforts and strategies to start converting affiliate links into sales. Your website must be a guiding tool for online users who are looking for products to satisfy their needs.

The real sense of affiliate marketing is not selling a product on your website but rather promoting products to get a successful buying decision. You'll be using your website to create quality content that promotes Amazon products.

a. How to Promote Amazon Products Effectively

First, be familiar with the important rules in promoting products online particularly with Amazon affiliate links.

1. Get active with your blog.

Your website will be the 'bread and butter' of your online business, so it requires valuable information for your visitors. Having regular quality contents on your website is a very good search engine optimization strategy. Google is able to see that your website is active with your added contents on a regular basis.

To maintain your affiliate marketing business, your blog must not be overly focused on a single product, otherwise, people will only know your site to be biased and out for money. If you promote too many products in a short period of time without providing other valuable information, you'll end up with no loyal followers.

Loyalty and trust from visitors need to be established beforehand. It becomes easier to get people and buy a product that you recommend if they trust you enough with what you're saying on your blog.

Getting active with your blog is the key to win people's trust. Practically, overkilling your content with affiliate links is a big NO!

2. Keep relevant products.

Look for products that focus on your niche market. Your affiliate links must be relevant products only. Think of products which are closely related to your niche.

Find products that can be useful to your niche and promote exactly how it was useful to you which brought you to recommend it to others.

3. Write interesting and honest reviews.

The best way to promote and make money with Amazon is to talk about your experience with certain products. Create in-depth reviews for your visitors.

Be honest when you write product reviews. The best way to give an honest review is to try the product. You may also ask someone else to try it for you. In doing so, you can be sure of the quality of the products you're promoting.

Write your review as simple as telling them your experience with the product. Mention some key facts like how you came across with the product, what are the features that delighted you most, and why others love it too.

You may also include the product's price and how you compare it to other products. But, there is a rule to maintain a balance of the product's pros and cons, so you may not sound like over promoting a product on your blog.

To make your content more interesting, write some buying tips and advice. Definitely, it makes sense to your readers.

Keep writing contents for people in a "buying mood." In the long run, your visitors will look at you as an expert in your small niche.

On the other hand, if you're just selling affiliate products on your blog, without giving valuable information to your readers, you won't generate sales from it. People visiting your blog will feel when you're only making some stories out of nowhere.

Make your content interesting and more visitors will get hooked with your posts.

4. Build affiliate links on your blog regularly.

It is advisable not to put many affiliate links in the first paragraph of your review or better have your first affiliate link in the second paragraph.

Here's what you can do. Use at least two links per post. Take note that a link to the end of your review has greater tendency to convert a sale when a visitor clicks your link after reading your review.

It is important that you keep note that Amazon links must have a no-follow attributes (use rel="nofollow") to avoid being penalized by Google.

Here's a simple guide on how to put Amazon affiliate link in your content.

• Log in to your Amazon account

• Find a product and look for the link "link to this page" text

• There will be 3 choices of links: (1) text and image (2) text only (3) image only

• Highlight the HTML code and copy it

- Go to your post and paste the code

Choosing which type of link to use depends on your preference and which will work best for your target market.

There is a tool to track your links when you create multiple affiliate tags. Initially, using different tags can help you compare any type of link and see which type of link generates sales on your blog.

Comparing each type of links, most people are drawn to buy a product if they see an image of the product. On the other hand, banner ads may be least effective for some to generate sales. Among the types of link, using a text link within the post is the common option to put affiliate links. It's preferable that when using a text link, edit the link text to avoid a long product title. Use a shortened text with two or three words for the product name.

Looking for a convenient way to build links on your website?

Try the WordPress plugin called Easy Azon. It makes it easy to add links. With the plugin, it enables searching and adding products from your WordPress Dashboard easily. It saves your time just by getting the product information and images for you.

Watch this YouTube video tutorial to help you start building affiliate links to promote Amazon products on your website.

YouTube Tutorial:
* **How to Insert Amazon Affiliate Links into your Blog Posts:** https://goo.gl/V8Jdxc

5. Proper article keywords are important.

Maintaining an active blog is not enough to keep promoting products on your website. Keyword strategy must be done properly to have your content be optimized for the search engine. Having a high search ranking creates more chance of people seeing your website.

Now, the efforts you started in finding your niche plays a big role in promoting products. Writing your post requires proper article keywords to get traffic.

And so, keyword research is necessary whenever you write content. Keywords should resemble the vocabulary of your target market. You need to think how your target market would think to identify keywords they will use in searching the web.

Just Google your proposed focus keyword and compare your article with the first two result pages if it has same keywords on their titles.

You may also look into the pages to decide on possible content ideas that may inspire you to include onto your blog.

Picking a focus keyword for your article is not easy. Take advantage of some tools that make your online business a bit easier. I have listed here the most useful tools in finding proper keywords namely:

- **Google Adwords Keyword Planner**- A tool that enables you to find new and related keywords without considering the search volume data. It helps you come up with potential keyword ideas. This is the same tool that is used in finding your niche.

  Google Adwords Keyword Planner: https://adwords.google.com/KeywordPlanner

- **Yoast Suggests** - A tool that gives a quick find of long tail keywords that uses the Google Suggest functionality. It enables keyword expansions from what Google suggests.

  Yoast Suggests: https://yoast.com/suggest/

- **Google Trends** - A tool that compares traffic of different sets of keywords, which also includes a comparison of various geographical regions.

  Google Trends: http://www.google.com/trends/

Aside from these tools, make use also of your internal search engine. Results of keywords that your actual visitors key in from your website that didn't get any results should be included on your keyword list. You may check the results of those keywords from Google Analytics, a WordPress plugin.

Doing keyword research will provide you list of relevant keywords that can help you better promote products on your website with the perfect keyword.

As you start promoting Amazon products on your blog by following the basic rules above, I encourage you to take advantage of Amazon's widgets. Installing widgets on your website will create a more engaging and enticing mood to your visitors. It allows you to promote products using interactive components installed on your website's sidebar or blog post.

Here are the steps on how to select a widget from Amazon Associates:

Step #1: Log in to your account at Amazon Associates.

Step #2: At the top of the homepage, click the "Widgets" tab. Display will show the available widgets (Search, Carousel, My Favorite widgets).

Step #3: Choose the widget you wish to add. Then, click the button, "Add to your Web page."

Step #4: Configure the widget by filling out the details needed for the widget you picked. This may take you some time to customize the widget from the Slideshow Widget screen.

Save as the widget. Then, click and copy the HTML code for the Amazon widget as displayed on the screen.

Step #5: In a new browser tab, go to your WordPress Dashboard, open the "Posts" section, click "Add New" and add the Amazon widget to a blog post. Click the HTML tab at the top of the editing screen. Then, click the part of your post where your widget needs to appear and paste the Amazon widget code by pressing "Ctrl-V."

If you wish to add the widget to the website sidebar, open the "Appearance" section and click "Widgets." Then, drag the "Text" widget from the list to the widget portion on the right side.

Step #6: Publish or save the widget by clicking "Publish" or "Save" button.

YouTube Tutorial:
- **Adding an Amazon Associate Widget:** https://goo.gl/SnRwt8

b. Blogging Tips to Maximize Your Sales

This is the stage that you will "plant, water, and nurture" your website, so your online business will bear fruits. It matters that you know and follow the rules in promoting products on your website.

Promoting products doesn't end with following the rules. The most difficult yet fulfilling part of promoting products on your blog is to make visitors feel the convenience when they visit your website. It's like a one-stop shop where everything they need will be answered just by reading your posts.

You'll be fulfilled when your website gets promoted through word of mouth or reviews of people who visited your blog. They can't help but share their great experience upon visiting your website. Your product should be as good as your content to create a perfect experience for your visitors that eventually translates to income.

To help you promote your blog and products you recommend, your creativity is a big plus in getting the right set of products for your blog. It may be a tough job to showcase the most appropriate products for your niche market.

And so, I have listed some content suggestions that you may include on your website to maximize sales from referred Amazon links.

1. List popular products.

Your visitors will find it convenient to see some lists of products that you recommend. Do this on a monthly or quarterly basis. Though you will be focusing on your niche, this can be an opportunity to introduce some related products or new topics. In this way, you can show your visitors how you value them by providing lists of popular products.

2. Offer seasonal content.

Your target market is expecting products from time to time especially on special occasions. Get this opportunity to post your recommended products for the season with the Amazon links.

The most awaited seasons are Christmas, Thanksgiving, Valentine's Day, and Halloween. You can research on other occasions of other countries if you want to target specific regions for a particular season.

3. Show the bestseller products.

People are interested to know the products that most people buy. They tend to buy products that most people are buying.

It's a human nature to follow and trust the majority, isn't it? Also, recommending the bestseller products on your blog is easier to promote because it's proven to be a saleable item.

4. Get promotional products with special offers or discounts.

Keep yourself updated with Amazon's special promotions that are related to your niche because it is a worthwhile content on your website. You may note on your post the discount it offers to catch the eye of your readers.

5. Encourage reader's reviews and comments.

When a reader sees other readers recommending the same as what your content is saying on your blog, your intent becomes more genuine. There is a tendency that more readers will be interested in trying the product. This strategy will also show how you value their opinions and can be a start of a conversation with your readers.

The sales you'll generate from affiliate links promoted on your blog will primarily come from converted loyalty and trust readership. Trust develops once your readers get connected with your blog on a regular basis. Remember that it takes readers to trust you enough to consider your recommendations on your blog. So, you have to ensure that your website contents are intended to build trust.

Your online business doesn't end with setting up your website, writing reviews, and putting affiliate links and widgets to promote Amazon products on your website. It requires more time and effort to be consistent and get the highest profit from it. Strategy to get traffic for your online business is another effort to make.

From the beginning of finding your niche to writing articles on your website, keywords you use must be well researched to gain traffic. In online business, traffic is considered an effective but difficult way to promote a product.

All internet marketers, who wish to make it big, compete for traffic on the web. And so, you must be ready to compete as well.

Getting traffic means getting exposure. No matter how well designed your blog is and how well thought your product reviews are, it will never reach your audience if you don't have traffic.

You'll need to learn some strategies to increase traffic, so online users will land on your pages and discover what your website has in store for them.

Here are some easy ways to start get traffic, be exposed and popular with your blog:

- Let your friends, families and acquaintances know about your blog

- Use your email to put your website link as part of your signature

- Create some video and leave a link at YouTube

- Be active in social media

I'd like to stress the importance of social media on your online business. Use your social media account to target a specific audience. You should post attention grabber headlines to promote your blog or introduce a recommended product.

Definitely, your social media accounts will play an essential role in promoting Amazon products. This is the reason why in building your website, it is advisable to create a social media account.

Getting traffic, being exposed and popular with your blog is not only promoting a recommended Amazon product to your visitors but also getting people in the door of Amazon in a relevant way.

Isn't it cool that you still get a commission from the purchases of referred visitors to Amazon even if it is not the product you promoted?

I'm sure that promoting products on your website will get more fun when you get to know more of your readers. More ideas will surely come your way.

Just keep in mind the product selection and blogging tips I shared with you so you can maximize your earning. These tips will ease any difficulty in maintaining your online business.

CHAPTER 6: 25 BEST KEPT SECRETS TO MAXIMIZE YOUR EARNINGS WITH AMAZON AFFILIATE PROGRAM

Hey, I would like to clear one question that may be on your mind. Is there a saturation point in doing an online business?

Any market may be saturated, but I think that web saturation is relative to time. It is more saturated as compared to previous days and tomorrow than today.

Despite web saturation through time, there are still tons of opportunities on the web especially for affiliate marketers.

At some point, I felt that the web already has too many sites with product advertisements on it. Indeed, the internet has become a channel to do business and not merely a source of information.

And so, more and more people are getting into affiliate marketing programs to make money online. This is a reason why it is very important to know and do all the best strategies to reach a high level performance in affiliate marketing.

Certainly, market saturation is inevitable. The ultimate key not to reach the saturation point is product diversity and unique website content.

If you would ask me, if Amazon Associate affiliate program offers the most diversified product lists and if you can create the most unique website for online users, my answer is a big YES!

And for you to do that, continue what you've started with your online business from Step 1 to 4 chapters of this book.

I really want you to succeed as an Amazon affiliate, and I believe you deserve to know the best kept secrets to maximize your earning with Amazon.

I know you've been waiting for this. Here are the secrets:

Secret #1: Start Early with Amazon.

The sooner you have a niche for your blog, write a few articles and start your affiliate marketing with Amazon. You'll be learning a lot of terms and features about it. And so, when you start early, you'll have much time to experiment to determine what features and strategies best fit on your blog.

Expect that before your website gets popular, it should have enough posts with affiliate links even if it will be converted into sales after some time.

Secret #2: Build Traffic.

Get noticed by building traffic to your website. Traffic translates to potential referred visitors to Amazon. Your website content will generate traffic for itself.

You'll get noticed if your content is valuable to online users, so write quality articles that are rich in content. A copied and pasted content from another website will not build you traffic because the search engine can detect contents that are not original, thus it will bring you to the bottom of the search results.

Keep your website fresh at any given time by writing articles frequently with variation in length. The average length of articles that get good traffic are those with around 1,600 words.

Posting of articles as frequent as six articles a week is also a traffic builder. You may make some variation on the length of your articles but be sure not to post an article that is too brief or too long.

Describe your article by having proper tags. Appropriate tags, description and metadata for your article helps in generating traffic when people search for articles that are related to your niche. Again, keywords play an important part in building traffic. Look for keywords and use it effectively.

You can select article keywords with less competition to have higher opportunity to drive traffic. You only need to ensure that the keywords you select are profitable and will give you higher conversion rates.

You have to practically make your website URL visible to many venues such as emails, forum, social media network where people can also easily share your website contents.

Secret # 3: Multiple Links to your Post.

There are affiliates who take the value of affiliate links for granted on their content. For them, having an affiliate link is good enough to earn a commission.

The secret of successful Amazon affiliates is having the thought that every link to their content is an opportunity for visitors to click and direct them to Amazon.

How would you do that as well?

Honestly, it's not too bad to have at least 5 to 10 links per post. If you have a long article, you can add some more links.

More so, you can link to your old post that is related to a current article.

Link building to other websites is another way to increase your presence on the web. Come up with good links by trading links with other websites related to your niche which you think can be useful to your visitors when landed on the pages.

Secret #4: Time Matters.

Time is a major factor in increasing earnings with Amazon affiliate program. Over the years of maintaining your website with continuous and regular posts with affiliate links, more loyal followers will come your way.

You need to research more on your niche to provide your visitors with appropriate information, but without putting affiliate links in every post you write.

You're not supposed to promote Amazon products in every post. You have to consider time in maintaining your website content with and without an Amazon affiliate links.

Another secret is to have the right timing to post reviews on products. You have to consider occasions as opportunity to keep your website updated and useful. Online users are definitely looking for products during occasions, so why not promote a product during holidays?

Secret #5: Get People onto Amazon.com.

As an Amazon affiliate, you only need to drive people to Amazon's site. Your referral links can do much for you to earn commission while Amazon takes care of your referred visitor to purchase on their site. They have designed techniques on their site to create sales from visitors.

Secret#6: Keep an Eye on Amazon.

Keep watching on what are products on sale at Amazon which are related to your niche and select the best products that you think your visitors need.

The secret is to regularly use Amazon so you can learn from them on how they promote products. They have designed their website perfectly for online users.

You can improve your website from what you see on Amazon such as using widgets, writing product description and using reviews to promote the products.

Secret #7: Promote High-Quality Products.

Blog readers appreciate reading posts that recommend high-quality products. In doing so, your readers will treat you professionally according to the quality of products you recommend. You'll find it fulfilling to give an honest review of products that passed high-quality criteria.

Secret #8: Product Images Affiliate Links.

Product image on blog is an asset to get some traffic. Most affiliate marketers consider product images with affiliate links as the second best way to convert sales, next to putting simple text on the content.

Do you know that readers have high tendency to click on images to get a closer look at it? Well, the secret is putting affiliate links with product images because it grabs the attention of visitors and encourages readers to click it.

Secret #9: Buy Now Button.

A secret button that conveniently directs the reader to buy a product that you promote. The image shows "Buy Now" text which has an Amazon affiliate link. Once clicked, your visitors will be directed to the Amazon cart where they can purchase the product.

Secret #10: Product Comparison List.

This is a comparison grid for all the products in your niche which will allow your visitors to sort different products and features. You may include a column for "buy now" button.

You can do this with WordPress Plugin, the *WP Table Reloaded*. Searching the products on the page will be easy for the readers.

Secret #11: Multiple Tracking ID.

With various ways to advertise and campaign your blog and products, tracking different methods is the secret. It will give you freedom to focus on what strategy, locations and products really convert into sales based on the tracker results.

Amazon assigns you with a tracking ID, but you can add up to 100 tracking IDs. Do not be too liberated to add tracking IDs for a short period of time.

The secret is to have only a few campaign strategies first before going into too many ways in determining where your traffic comes from.

Secret#12: Small Ticket Items.

It's relatively acceptable to promote small ticket items on your blog. One sale of an inexpensive product can make you one step higher to the next bracket with higher commission rate.

That's right! Just add up large quantities of inexpensive products to your niche and it will help you reach higher percentage commission rate brackets.

Remember the illustration I showed how Amazon rewards affiliates? Your commission percentage rate depends on the number of products purchased by your referred visitors.

Typically, reviewing products that are less expensive are most likely to convert a sale, especially when your target market is budget conscious.

Secret #13: Email List.

Freebies make your readers happy. The secret of affiliates is building an email list so they can offer some freebie to followers. Freebies like buyer's guide or any information that interests your readers make a more personal approach in communicating with followers.

Likewise, you can take advantage of the holidays by sending them a newsletter. There are newsletter providers on the web that you may use like **Aweber**.

Aweber: *www.aweber.com/*

Providing email subscription option on your website gives the power to build a list of potential customers of Amazon.

Secret #14: Target Localized Market.

Affiliates can promote Amazon products locally. When you have identified where your traffic is coming from, you can promote products from the local Amazon that your visitors come from.

To do this, check the countries where Amazon ship products that are related to your niche. Then, try to localize your website.

You may also consider putting two different links in one post to promote products in two different countries if your website shows traffic to various regions.

Secret #15: Use Contextual links.

In writing a product review, incorporate a contextual link on your content. It is a secret and proven strategy that has a high probability of converting a link into a sale.

With a contextual link, it tells more about the product if your reader sees a link within your post as compared to using banners on the sidebar. When readers want to know more about what you're talking about in your post, there is a higher chance that a link will be clicked. And this link is your affiliate link to Amazon.

Secret # 16: Write Bestselling List Post.

Amazon is regularly providing a list of suggested products that are best-selling. It is wise to write a review of bestselling products related to your niche. Bestselling products have a greater rate of conversion if you promote it on your blog.

Secret #17: Get More Related Products.

The secret is to make yourself be an expert in your niche. You can do this by introducing more related products and recommend it on your blog.

When readers see a personal touch from your product review, it helps them decide to buy.

Getting more products doesn't mean promoting them at the same time. Keep a balance of reviewing three to seven products at a time, then post your article on your website. Again, select some products with special discounts or promotion to boost your income.

Secret #18: Consider Digital Products.

The convenience of having digital products to offer is that no shipment is necessary. Downloadable products such as books, apps, games, and music are most likely to convert into sales.

Research if your niche can have both a digital and physical product which you can promote. If there is none, you can create and produce a digital product, just to get more visitors on your website.

Secret#19: Make Buying Guides.

A buying guide on your blog will create an easy buying ambiance for your readers. Give them the best options and provide pertinent information on the products. Your buying guide should showcase the features, advantages and disadvantages of each product they can choose from.

When a first-time visitor reads your blog and sees that your buying guide is a good help, that visitor can be a loyal follower. And, visiting your website becomes the source of advice when planning to buy a new product.

Secret #20: Readers Matter the Most.

The intent of your website is to address the reader's problems and needs. You have to come up with products that can answer their needs.

If a reader happens to search your topic, it should make the reader feel that they have found the right authority to get the information they need.

The secret is to make sure that you sound natural when reviewing or recommending a product. You can only do this if you know the product well and you understand your target market.

You need to listen to the buyers and determine the other interests of your readers if any. Do this by checking on your Earning Report. You can see the products which you didn't promote on your website but your referrals purchased from Amazon.

From that report, you'll have a better idea what matters to your readers. It's up to you to think of ideas how you can include other products related to the interests of your readers without getting out from your niche.

Secret #21: Price is Not the First Priority.

Considering the price of the products is only a matter of strategy but not necessarily the first priority in choosing the products to promote. You can do well for both promoting a big and small ticket items at the same time.

I have shared with you the advantages of having the big tickets items as well as the small ticket items.

You may have the combination of both, but at some point, you need to focus on which set of items gives you the biggest commission.

It's true that a big ticket item may give big commission instantly; that's why most affiliate marketers go for big ticket items. In that case, there is higher competition on these items because of too many websites promoting items with at least $100 price.

On the other hand, it can be more practical to promote a smaller ticket item because it has a potential to earn you same money or greater amount compared to big ticket items.

How is it possible? Since the products are inexpensive, buyers have a tendency to buy in bulk or get some other products on Amazon to avail free shipping. Thus, it increases the total purchased amount and qualifies you also to a higher commission rate bracket in a month when more products are purchased from your referred links.

As an Amazon affiliate, considering the price is considered to be least important. There are other factors which have greater impact on your earning.

The next secrets I have for you will help you select the products to promote to maximize your earning with Amazon affiliate program.

Secret # 22: Look for "Evergreen" Products.

Take note that for as long as your website is active, your archives can still result in a successful referral even after some years. Given the possible opportunities in the future, you have to consider not promoting the "hot items" only.

Think of items that can interest people even after 2 to 10 years or more. You must think it long term so your single effort to write a review and link it to Amazon will earn you for a long time. It's only a matter of looking into the "evergreen" products to promote.

Secret # 23: 5 Star Reviews is a Plus.

There will be times that affiliates find it difficult to look for products to promote or how to promote a product. One secret they do is to look for products with 5 Star Reviews.

Your review will be in accordance to the customer reviews who actually bought the product. Do it, if you or anyone you know can't use the product to provide a first-hand experience to make a review.

Of course, search for items that are related to your niche. It is considerable to have at least 5 customers who reviewed the product. Nonetheless, a 4-star review can be the least you can consider when choosing a product.

Secret #24: Search Top sellers within a Smaller Niche.

Top sellers on Amazon are available for your view and you can get potential items to promote on your website.

However, when you select items from this list, you'll have difficulty to get traffic. Why? Simply because these are highly popular items and competition can be very high.

The secret to being able to compete and take advantage of the top sellers is to search the most popular items which belong to the smaller niche market that is somehow related to your website

Secret # 25: Promote Products you Love and Used.

You know that Amazon has a lot of products to sell and you have more products you need as well. Whatever product you love and you practically use is the first selection criteria you can have.

Definitely, there are products that you may need at any time and once you've tried a product from Amazon and loved the product, it's a signal that you better promote it on your website.

It's fulfilling to write a review and promote the products that you love and personally used. By reviewing such products, you'll be sharing your experience with your readers.

Wow! Isn't it great?

There are overflowing ideas to make your earnings get higher.

Another thing, you can also have a global reach if you choose to promote your affiliate links on the internet properly and thus you will have the higher probability of a greater income. Nothing is impossible if you work on it!

Well, you seem to get the most of your online business without producing your own products. Every secret I shared will actually help you get into affiliate marketing and succeed as an Amazon affiliate.

Truly, being an Amazon affiliate may be the cheapest and quickest way to start an online business and make money.

Keep in mind that Amazon plays an important part in your online business. And, with its long years of existence, Amazon has established the widest venue for products to promote and more features to generate commissions from their products.

And that brings me to share with you another secret.

In fact, most of WordPress bloggers are monetizing their blog through adding another Amazon page. It's the Amazon aStore, and it can increase your passive income.

How does Amazon aStore differ from promoting products with Amazon affiliate links?

The difference is that you can design a website page effectively and fast by adding default aStore design with a little matching of colors with your WordPress theme.

With aStore on your website, you'll be promoting a product without writing a product review or article. Amazon aStore is simply an add-on page on your website dedicated to a number of products that you recommend to your visitors.

On the page, you can include a list of your popular and recent posts, categories, and archives, as well a preview of About the Author, a Contact Form, and put relevant information on the sidebar.

How does aStore make a quick method in promoting products?

The aStore widget on Amazon has easy steps to follow once you have signed up with Amazon Associates. Just log on to your Amazon account and the aStore tab will guide you to incorporate an aStore onto your website.

This short video tutorial on YouTube entitled **How to add an Amazon aStore to WordPress to increase passive income** (https://goo.gl/nKe1ns) will show you how fast and easy it is to add aStore on your website. Just click on the title and watch the video.

Amazon and WordPress offer various tools and techniques to make your online business easy to handle. Take advantage of the resources available to you.

Use these secrets to your full advantage.

I intend to share the best-kept secrets to you so that you'll know better when you start promoting products on your website.

CHAPTER 7: 11 BEST PRACTICES HOW NOT TO GET BANNED ON AMAZON ASSOCIATES

Okay, you now know what to do to become an Amazon affiliate.

I have this chapter for you to disclose what you should NOT DO once you become an Amazon Affiliate.

Of course, I would not want you to build a well-designed website, select the most profitable products, get the highest number of readers, and earn high commission, and then-wake up one morning and realize you have been banned from Amazon Associates and worse: you'll not be getting the payment left from your account.

Yes, you read it right. You can be banned from Amazon, even with a minor and unintentional action you make. So, I advise you to take this seriously and read on.

1. Don't forget to read the Amazon Associates Operating Agreement.

I consider this as the most important reminder to any Amazon Affiliate. When you signed up, you have confirmed that you agree to the terms and condition of the program. Therefore, you have to follow it. So, never forget to read the Operating Agreement very thoroughly including the links to additional information.

It will guide you on how to be an Amazon Affiliate and what is the program all about. There could be updates from time to time, and so you must not disregard it. You must notify Amazon whenever you have changed your email address to ensure that you're not missing any notifications from Amazon.

When you read the agreement, you get to familiarize with the program, the rights of Amazon and the type of relationship you'll have with Amazon.

You can check it at **https://affiliate-program.amazon.com/gp/associates/agreement** for reference. You have to dig on every detail of it.

Definitely, reading it won't be a waste of time at all.

2. Don't put affiliate links on websites you don't own.

When you signed up with Amazon Associates, you provided them with your website information. This means that they approved your account according to the information you provided. Thus, don't put your affiliate links to websites you don't own. Because when you do so, spammers will be prevented from getting sales using malwares. Otherwise, a spammy behavior of putting your affiliate links on third-party websites may lead you to the Amazon's list of banned accounts.

3. Don't misrepresent your Amazon affiliation.

What do I mean by this, exactly? You must be aware that Amazon requires every affiliate to clearly state that you're part of the affiliate program on each page that has Amazon affiliate links.

You should not be hiding that you're indeed an Amazon Affiliate. To ensure that you're representing Amazon properly, include the disclosure statement below on every page that has Amazon link on your website.

"[Insert your name] is a participant in the Amazon Services LLC Associates Program, an affiliate advertising program designed to provide a means for sites to earn advertising fees by advertising and linking to [insert the applicable site name (amazon.com, amazonsupply.com, or myhabit.com)]."

You may consider putting the statement at the footer of the webpage which is the most recommended area on the website.

4. Don't copy and paste reviews or comments from Amazon.

As an Amazon Affiliate, the information you get from Amazon is through an affiliate link. And so, you're not allowed to just copy and paste information like reviews or comments directly from Amazon.

5. Don't cheat Amazon's system by using IFRAME on your site.

Iframe is one of the techniques in cookie stuffing where a page is embedded within a page, with one simple line of code. It enables to update parts of a website while the user browses without reloading the whole page.

Affiliates embed an iframe onto their page that includes their affiliate URL, which shows as if Amazon or any part of it is embedded within its site. Amazon doesn't allow iframing when done as cookie stuffing that cheats the Amazon's 24-hour cookie period regulation as the basis of commissions from referred links.

There is no way that you can't be caught cheating by doing cookie stuffing. It's a practice of dropping affiliate cookies on user's computer without actually clicking on an affiliate link or knowing that they are accepting the cookie. Cookie stuffing is one of the common reasons why Amazon bans an affiliate.

For example, a user visits a website and it results to receive a third-party cookie from an entirely different website which is the target affiliate website. Then, if the user visits the target website, clicks on the affiliate link and makes a transaction, the cookie stuffer is paid a commission. Thus, it generates illegitimate affiliate sales.

Surely, Amazon has their means to identify websites that do cookie stuffing. By doing this, the affiliate who owns the website will be banned from Amazon.

However, Amazon has special links that require iframes, for example getting a link on Reviews from Amazon. You will not be banned by iframing for as long as your links are in accordance with Amazon's Operating Agreement.

6. Don't use unclear links.

Your participation to Amazon Associate Affiliate Program is requiring your links to Amazon site to be not confusing or misleading. When your website is reviewed to contain links to Amazon that are improperly labeled, then, Amazon considers your links to be sending an unclear message on it.

Amazon requires affiliates to comply with a clear notation that a link is actually a link to Amazon website. Don't use URL shortener to hide any other motives for linking a certain product, making it unclear to show your link as a link to Amazon site.

For you to avoid unclear links, you may use Amazon's link shortening service, the *amzn.to* through **http://bit.ly**.

Bit.ly is a free URL shortening service which also offers real-time analytics that enables you to see how many clicks your links get. It automatically formats link Amazon URLs to a short *amzn.to* link.

It is as simple as copying the product link URL from your Amazon account and pasting it into the "Shorten Links Here" input box on Bitly.com homepage. Then, click the "Shorten" button and you'll get instantly the shortened *amzn.to* link.

Since Amazon affiliate link is somewhat very long, you have to be very careful with URL shortening services because when to do it in an unclear manner, it may be a ground to ban you from Amazon. So, when you shorten your affiliate URL, make sure to use the Amazon shortener service provider.

7. Don't promote affiliate links in any offline manner.

Most bloggers seem to do some misleading manner of promoting products with Amazon affiliate links. Keep in mind that you can promote a product with Amazon special links on your own website only.

Amazon doesn't permit any offline manner of promotion using your direct affiliate links. It includes promoting links in email, newsletter, printed materials, SMS, mailing, MMS, attachment to an email or RSS feeds.

And so, always read this practical tip before putting Amazon affiliate links outside your website to make sure that you'll not get banned to what you're about to do.

8. Don't operate more than one account.

Technically speaking, affiliates are only allowed to have one Amazon account. Don't try to create another one or more unless you apply to Amazon for a special exception.

You're lucky if you can be one of the website owners that Amazon can allow to legitimately have more than one account.

9. Don't' link from an unsuitable website.

During sign up with the Amazon Associate Affiliate Program, your website is evaluated in terms of the suitability of your website contents. Once approved, your website must remain as such.

Don't intend to promote or contain sexually explicit, violent, and libelous or defamatory materials as well as employing discrimination, or undertaking illegal activities because these are unsuitable sites for Amazon.

10. Don't promote counterfeit products.

Amazon is not permitting an affiliate to violate intellectual property rights. And so, your website should not contain fake products.

Don't ever think that Amazon tolerates a website that promotes counterfeit products providing the lower price of a brand. Amazon is making sure that special links to Amazon come from legitimate contents.

11. Don't redirect affiliate links to other sales process.

As a general Amazon guideline, you must not attempt to divert transactions or buyers away from Amazon.com. You're not supposed to use Amazon links to redirect users for other purposes other than promoting Amazon and its products within Amazon site.

Any advertisements, marketing messages or "calls to action" that may lead or encourage Amazon users to leave Amazon.com are prohibited.

One way to keep away from being banned is not to redirect an affiliate link using an email and inclusion of hyperlinks and web addresses that will divert buyers to other sales process.

For some Amazon affiliates, it may be terrifying to be banned without prior notice, and that is the reason why it matters to have an in-depth understanding of Amazon Associates' guidelines and policies.

I advise you that whenever there is ambiguity on any part of the Amazon Operating Agreement, don't hesitate to email Amazon and ask some clarifications. Amazon is still the best resource you can get as compared to getting it from other bloggers who share their Amazon experience.

The best practices have just been revealed to you.

Be confident!

You're sure to start your online business with the most proven ways to earn money as an Amazon affiliate.

CONCLUSION

This is the end of my book. I'm excited for you! This could be the start of your successful life with affiliate marketing through this Amazon Associates Bible.

I started writing this book hoping that you'll be guided on how to earn money online. And I would like to end this book with a hope that you're now equipped to be a successful Amazon affiliate with your online business.

Maybe at some point, the guide is overwhelming. I won't deny that it can be at some point in doing the actual tasks. But, it shouldn't hinder you to pursue the online business unless you want to be left behind.

As you can see, the internet is growing fast. And so, timing is essential for affiliate marketing to succeed. Your niche could be the next top ranking site years from now if you choose to create your website immediately.

Take advantage of this book and walk through every step of it, from finding your niche to promoting Amazon products. Don't rush it. Just enjoy each step and get a great experience as you do it with passion.

The more effort and time in preparing your business, the stronger your foundation will be.

This book is packed with practical tips and I encourage you to review it several times. Try to explore and practice it as soon as possible.

If you have questions not covered in this book and you wish to dig deeper with it, you can do more research about it as this book can only cover the basics. It's important that you research more into ideas that matter most to you in order to be successful.

You can also leave a comment on the review section if you want to suggest a topic that you want me to cover in the next edition of this e-book.

And also, don't be alarmed by the idea of getting banned from Amazon and how Amazon strictly regulates the affiliates. One good thing about this is that people learn from the experience of others.

By following the best practices as an Amazon affiliate, you can be spared from getting banned and be at peace while promoting Amazon products. Why? Because you already know the dos and don'ts, thanks to this book.

Remember, as an affiliate, agreeing to the affiliate program's terms and condition means a clear understanding of it. Following the agreement is a necessary action. If you choose the other way, you must be ready to take the consequences of being banned.

I hope it won't happen to you because this book aims to guide you to do the proper way. Reading this book is not the only proper way of starting a business with affiliate marketing, but this is the first step. Even long-time affiliate marketers experienced failures before reaching a high-income stream, and many still fail up to this time. Thus, this book doesn't guarantee a hassle-free online business.

When you bought this book, I'm sure you were looking for resources that could answer your need to make money online. Or should I guess? It's because of curiosity on how to earn with Amazon affiliate program. Whatever is your reason for getting this book, your fulfillment lies on the action you'll make.

I wrote this book to provide a good resource on how to make money online with Amazon Associates affiliate program. Consume this by doing what is supposed to do. Read again the whole book if needed, but act on it the soonest possible. It is better to start now rather than to delay or do nothing at all. I believe a good resource is well consumed when it results in greater productivity.

Now you have a complete guide to making money online with Amazon. Don't waste it. Go ahead and practice it now, this is not the time to procrastinate. It will bear fruits at the right time if you start today and nurture it properly.

Persevere and be patient because this could be a lifetime journey which can earn you a living.

I'm telling you, you're one step ahead to your success. So, act and plan your next step TODAY.

The best **TIME** to start is **NOW!**

Leave a Book Review

Tell me what you think
Did you learn something from this book? Tell other readers what you think about this book by leaving a book review.

Write a review: https://goo.gl/uhFKrv

My New Book

Hi, Friend!

I just released a new and more advanced book called **Amazon FBA: Complete Expert Guide.** This book tackles more **secrets** on *how you can Private Label your products, how to deal with the manufacturers,* and *how to grow your Amazon FBA business.* It will be helpful if you could also purchase this book for your own study and reference since this book deals with more advanced topics in more detail.

Amazon FBA: Complete Expert Guide book page:
http://goo.gl/Gs7ZJt

Once again, thank you for purchasing this book. And as a token of thanks, I'm giving you, for FREE, the first chapter of my new book. Have a wonderful reading. Thanks a lot!

– Dan Johnson.

Book Description

Amazon FBA is the answer to the problem that all online sellers undergo. With Amazon FBA, you can achieve a consistent and swift shipping service that you do not need to bother with. They do all the picking, packing, shipping and many more processes for you! What about the warehousing space? Well, they cover that as well.

Imagine. All this information placed in one book.

This book does not only solve the problem encountered with shipping services or warehousing services. It also dives into every aspect you should consider with every product. From which products you should consider selling, international markets you can sell in, placing you in the search engine even as a new seller, tips on promoting your products and even the right way to price your products so there's no chance of bankruptcy.

With the use of this Amazon FBA e-book, you have stumbled on the best how-to; guidebook there is to increase your selling experience and success rate to the maximum level!

Amazon FBA is the ultimate guide for online sellers, both for the already established substantial and highly reputable retail firms, for the little, just-started online retail stores and everything in between.

It is based on the opportunity of selling your products online through the use of Fulfillment by Amazon, otherwise known as Amazon's FBA. Amazon, the genius that they are, has come up with a brilliant way in aiding your insufficient online business in becoming the best of the best! They pack, pick and ship all your products that your customers have ordered to lessen your headache.

Letting this opportunity go may lose your opportunity in beating the competitor's that you have dreamed of surpassing. The long awaited ultimate book to success in online selling has arrived.

CHAPTER 1: WHAT IS FULFILLMENT BY AMAZON (FBA)?

So what is this game-changing way of selling your products you ask?

Amazon has been able to innovate and create one of the most advanced fulfillment networks in the world, with the smart idea of contributing to help other people's businesses in the process.

It's a service that basically has Amazon store the products that you sell in their fulfillment centers.

They will be able to do everything from picking, packing and shipping your product with provided customer services.

This has supported so many businesses already, as it helps you scale your business and be able to reach the customers you weren't able to before. A survey was done in 2014 showing that 71% of FBA respondents have reported that their unit sales have increased to 20% more on Amazon.com once they have joined.

This can help your business too.

Let's take this example:

Back in the day, if you wanted to ship items to your customers, you would have to do it one at a time rather than all at once. This meant that as business and sales got better, then you would have to hire employees and more warehouse space. Basically, you'd have a headache.

What Fulfillment by Amazon had done, is that they had taken away all the headache of past problems and provided a simple solution to the problem: *You will ship your products in bulk to Amazon and Amazon will be the ones to pack and ship each individual order that you have received for you*

Isn't that amazing?

That Isn't The Only Benefit Of FBA

But, simply disposing of the headache of shipping isn't any different to all the other fulfillment centers out there that provide the same service Amazon does.

Now you're asking: *What's the big deal with Amazon's fulfillment centers then?*

Well, you don't just have all your products in one place and being shipped for you, but your sales will definitely jump, not just sissy kids jump, but like really a jump when in the use of FBA.

Why Does Sales Increase?

The reason your sales increase when using Amazon's FBA is that now your products can qualify under the Amazon's Free Super Saver Shipping. This basically means that Amazon will be able to offer to your customer free shipping when there is a purchased done over $25

It's not over because Amazon will also be able to offer their Amazon Prime members Free, Two-day shipping on all of your products.

Now, if you think about it, as you are shopping online do you think you would prefer to buy from a seller that is able to offer you a 2-day shipping for Free? People would die for that 2-day Free Shipping. If it weren't there, there would be more of a chance that your customers would just pass on your products. In the end, most of your potential customers would be passing, due to the hassle of adding shipping fee and long shipping time.

Fulfillment by Amazon is able to remove this hurdle along with your headache.

This Business Does Not Sleep

Since Amazon has the responsibility of shipping your products to all your customers, it has to work 24 hours a day in order to make sure that your orders go out fast and can be delivered on time to customers.

You are able to even go on vacation and your business will be able to run on autopilot for you, orders will be able to come in and products will go out as you sip on that Pina Colada.

A Growing Internet Business

Instead of attaining the expensive warehouse space that you need and all the employees you need to hire in order to ship your orders, you are able to work at home and be able to ship your products to Amazon in bulk.

You know what? You can even have any imported goods shipped directly to the Amazon fulfillment centers.

This type of business model allows you to grow rapidly without the need for all the tremendously expensive warehouse space and equipment that would add on to the costs of your business.

You are also able to use this model as a way to manage and ship the orders that your customers have placed in other online markets such as eBay, Buy.com, and others.

What Are The Products That You Are Allowed To Ship To Amazon?

Amazon may have started out as an online outlet for selling books, but it has definitely improved how it was before.

People can now buy jewelry, lawnmowers, beds, electronics and even exercise equipment. You want it; just name it.

You have the ability to ship even media items like books and non-media items like toys, home or garden items and much, much more.

The Fulfillment By Amazon Fees

The Fulfillment by Amazon fees are considerably low, which makes it definitely beneficial for those who have just started out in this business.

The fees may be updated from time to time and change, but the following are what you could expect:

- Fee for Picking (Per Order) = Approximately $1

- Fee for Packing (Per Order) = Approximately $1

- Weight-based Fee (Per Order) = Approximately $0.40 for every pound being shipped to a customer

- Storage Fee = Approximately $0.45 for every cubic foot of storage space that you may need to attain

- Inbound Freight = What it may cost you to ship your products to Amazon

- What's great about inbound freight fee is that Amazon will support you by partnering you up with them on shipping; this means that you will be able to use their shockingly low shipping rates.

All you have to do is to tell Amazon how big and heavy your package will be and the website will produce a label for you to be able to place on your box.

Easy and Simple, don't you think?

To see Amazon FBA's latest fee charges, please check **FBA Fulfillment Fees** page.

FBA Fulfillment Fees page: http://goo.gl/wi1d8g

Does FBA Work Only For People Working From Home?

Of course not!

There are even businesses that have already been in the business of selling online and had already been able to sell thousands upon thousands of products in their online stores even though they weren't using FBA. After joining the FBA program, their sales and business had increased tremendously.

Is It Possible To Have A Right And A Wrong Way To Use FBA?

Yes, there is.

This is more in the sense that there are strategies that would definitely help your business when using the FBA tactic and there are strategies that would just bring your business down.

Here's an example:

It would be most unfortunate for you and your business if you had decided to purchase vast amounts of products and ship it to the Amazon fulfillment centers just to realize that numerous amounts of other people have already done the same thing you did.

You need to be able to think strategically when you come into this business; you can't just go in blindly.

Ask yourself this: '*What can you and your business provide that no one else has already?*' or '*What can you sell to be unique from all the other businesses?*'

If you want to be able to achieve the different from the usual, then list all the products you have noticed that has not already been in the FBA and you will be able to benefit immensely if you are able to follow this strategy.

Once you take a look at the products that no one else is selling then you are able to sell your products without the worry of the competition within your online market.

Make sure you look for those items that differentiate you from the rest and can be considered desirable to all your potential customers and you will be able to gain so much more sales than you could have ever considered gaining.

a. Reasons To Choose Amazon For Selling

There are numerous other online markets to sell from, Amazon and eBay are two examples. They are both highly successful platforms for selling although they have differences in their operation, shopping experience.

Sellers may get confused as to where and who to go to sell, here's a quick guide as to why choosing Amazon would be most advantageous to your business compared to the rest.

1 - Elegance And Simplicity

Amazon has a very simplistic and organized selling platform in the industry. Comparing Amazon and the other online selling platforms, the others may have a longer process to go through just to get selling. Amazon's web store interface is also elegant and simple to use which will make your buyer's shopping experience a more enjoyable one.

2 - Attaining Fulfillment Without The Hassle

When using another online market platform, it would be up to you as the seller to see that your buyer gets what they paid for. This basically means that you will either have to create and maintain relationships between fulfillment partner(s) or that you would have to handle your own fulfillment (all the inventory, packaging, and shipping) all on your own.

When in Amazon, you can use their Fulfillment by Amazon, just send everything to Amazon with no cost and let them deal with your headache.

3 - Reduced Overhead

The way Amazon has created its system does not just provide the fulfillment platform, but it allows provides the opportunity to reduce their overhead expenses.

Since, in Amazon, you don't need to produce your own listing or continuously re-list your items on Amazon. Your maintenance overhead levels, as time goes by, will reduce.

The same things happen for the communication time since the buyers and sellers rarely need any communication.

4 - Better Visibility As A Smaller Seller

As a seller that may be just starting out in an online marketing platform, you may be one of those people buried at the end of the search list and covered by all those top-sellers or those that high-level feedbacks due to the innovation of the best match search system.

What Amazon does is that they have created a system that when buyers are searching for an item, the sellers that are shown are rotated. This allows for the new sellers to gain exposure. Since the buyers that go to Amazon, don't technically need to evaluate the sellers then there is almost always guaranteed sale.

5 - Be Where The Industry Has Growth

The online marketplace platform of Amazon has been growing much more rapidly year-by-year than that of any other online marketplace platforms is growing.

So, if you want to be in action then Amazon is for you.

From what this chapter has mentioned, Amazon has a lot to offer than that of any other online marketing platforms.

However, Amazon isn't for everyone; we all have our own dissenting opinions on its operation. But here are just a couple of points that will help you contemplate on the possible advantages you can reap from Amazon.

Amazon isn't Amazon today without the immense marketing and advertising strategies; a pinnacle of technological commerce in the modern era. Amazon is growing in consumers and members each day reaching out to various parts of the globe. One of the apparent benefits of selling on Amazon is the millions of people and markets it is currently attracting. It presents you with open access to sell your products in all five Amazon marketplaces in the safety of your home. There are more chances of you selling your product here than at the local mart. More exposure, more consumers, more money.

It's completely understandable that you're just not used to doing things online and prefer more tangible methods of earning money. However, everyone is using Amazon to expand their business horizons, either surf the wave of revenue or be attached to traditional concepts of business. Amazon is constantly upgrading to keep up with the dynamic world.

It's not to say that you should immediately shut your website or store or any personal retail outside of Amazon; the situation is relative.

If your website offers more income to your pockets, then so be it. Nevertheless, Amazon will give you, even more, opportunities on top of your standard income.

The idea of it excites you, otherwise, you wouldn't be reading about what you can benefit from Amazon. There's no costly rent in comparison to tangible stores, you don't even need to worry about location. You can save the hassle of marketing your products and have people familiarize your brand. As long as you follow these rules and have the ethical and positive approach to this business, you're good to go.

Perhaps you doubt the faithfulness of the people you transact with; scammers, fraud and all. Have no fear. Amazon's security is something it should boast with novel ways of protecting you and your customers - from strict regulations on timely payments to traceable shipment. Disobedience to the rules will either lower your status to make it difficult to conduct business or ban you completely. Amazon has little tolerance to fraudulent schemes to create a protected working environment for all.

You may think that the added fees on top of your products don't leave you enough room for profit. You may believe that in the end, you'll be the one making a loss. I beg to differ. Amazon has generated components to make it as trouble-free as possible. Features, like the fixed price of the Pro Merchant Subscriptions, actually gives you a heads up on your expenses calculations. The Fulfillment by Amazon (FBA) offers a great deal of ways to increase your sales, customer service available in the local language and Amazon warehouses that stores your products for you. It's a win-win situation.

b. How Does It Work?

Now you have an idea of what Fulfillment by Amazon is and the numerous amounts of benefits that it can provide for you and your business.

How exactly does it work? The way that Fulfillment by Amazon works has been mentioned previously, although, we will now go on an in-depth explanation of how it goes about its process.

In simple words: **Your business sells the items and Amazon ships it.**

Here are steps on how to use the FBA:

STEP #1: Send All Your Products To Amazon

All of the products from new to used are first sent to Amazon's fulfillment centers.

Here are the sub-steps provided to proceed to send your products to Amazon's fulfillment centers.

- You can do this by first uploading your listings to the Seller Central

- After that, you allow Amazon to fulfill either all or part of your inventory listing

- Print the PDF labeling either provided by Amazon or you can use the Fulfillment by Amazon's label service

- Use the discounted shipping that Amazon provides or you can select your own carrier of choice.

STEP #2: Amazon Will Store All Your Products

Once all your products have been sent to Amazon, they will then catalog your items and store your products in their ready-to-ship inventory

This is how it works:
- Once Amazon has received your products, they will then scan your inventory

- Unit dimensions are then provided to be able to accommodate the storage space needed

- For those who want to monitor their inventory placed in the Amazon's fulfillment center, there is an integrated tracking system established by Amazon.

STEP #3: Customers Will Place Orders For Your Products

Customers who have placed orders directly on Amazon will be fulfilled by Amazon.

- Your listings on Amazon will be ranked by the prices presented with no shipping costs added since those items are entitled to free shipping for purchases that are over $35*.

- For those customers on Amazon Prime*, they can upgrade their shipping options in order to eligible FBA listings.

* This excludes multi-channel fulfillment orders that have been placed on other websites and services that include Amazon Webstore or the Checkout by Amazon.

STEP #4: Amazon Will Be The Ones To Pick And Pack Your Products

The products for sale that have been ordered by customers will be picked and packaged for delivery

This is how it works:
- Amazon will be the one to locate your products through the use of advanced web-

to-warehouse, high-speed picking and a sorting system that Amazon has developed

- Customers are allowed to combine different ordered with other products that have been fulfilled by Amazon

STEP #5: Amazon Then Ships Your Products To The Customers

Amazon will then be able to ship the products the customers have requested through their network of fulfillment centers

This is how it works:
- Amazon will choose whichever method is comfortable for them for shipping

- Tracking information is provided for the customers

- For orders placed on Amazon.com, customers are able to contact customer's services for any inquiries.

YouTube Video Tutorials
- **How Fulfillment by Amazon (FBA) works:** https://goo.gl/cRWhEE
- **Tour of Fulfillment by Amazon (FBA):** https://goo.gl/1D6usZ
- **How Amazon Receives Your Inventory:** https://goo.gl/CAAYgH
- **Amazon FBA - What It Is And How it Works!:** https://goo.gl/smjfN8
- **How to Start an Online Business on Amazon the RIGHT way with no Technical Knowledge:** https://goo.gl/R8xBZu

c. Why Is FBA a Big Deal?

With all the big buzz of Fulfillment by Amazon, some sellers may be wondering: FBA is just another fulfillment method, isn't it? What's all this talk about the use of FBA? Basically, **What's the big deal about FBA?**

FBA becomes a big deal once you realize the amount of support it can place on your online business. For some, it becomes a **major decision** in their business in terms of profit that they will be making during their online career.

Those who may get to feel the best effect of the FBA are those who are small business owners, these people may not have the most efficient fulfillment systems in their arsenal and may not want to risk any potential negative effects from a poor customer experience.

Although there is plenty amounts of benefits that a seller can gain from using FBA, you should also never forget the following:

- Not every third-party seller should use FBA; it all really depends on the individual seller's financial resources as well as the nature of his or her business.

- Sellers should look at FBA as another weapon in their arsenal and not as a blanket resource. Sellers should either be 100% FBA or 100% FBM (Fulfillment by Merchant), although most professional sellers have become a hybrid of both

- Not all the products that have been submitted for FBA will end up being a good candidate for a number of reasons, mainly size, performance of their sales and their margin.

d. How FBA affects Product Discoverability and Buyability?

Before we get into learning on how FBA affects product Discoverability and Buyability, we will first look into the two terms:

1. Discoverability

This is the ability for your product listing to be found on Amazon. Amazon focuses on the type of search results on the different products rather than the type of seller

When it comes to having people be able to reach your products, FBA products are indeed the ones who get more discoverable for two reasons:

Reason #1: Amazon Prime Members

Prime members are those who spend more time shopping on Amazon than the average customer. These customers are entitled to filtering out all the non-Prime offers, which basically takes away those products that aren't in the FBA listing system.

Reason #2: Amazon's Reputation

Even if your product does by chance show up on the shoppers list, there will be items that will possess the offer that shows '*Fulfillment by Amazon*' and are more desirable for customers due to the efficient and traceable delivery process

2. Buyability

A product's likelihood of being bought or in more actionable terms, this is the product's chance of winning the Buy Box

Here are the effects on Buyability:

Reason #1: Seller's Rating

FBA sellers will not gain any negative ratings on the metrics of On-Time Delivery Rate and Late Shipment Rate due to FBA.

Reason #2: Fulfillment Latency

FBA items are instantly placed in the shortest latency windows, while FBM offers might proceed to be in longer windows (ex. 3-4 business days)

---

e. Advantages of Amazon FBA

Using Fulfillment by Amazon offers huge benefits for sellers like you. Here are the best benefits you can get by using Amazon FBA:

1-Accessibility to the Prime Members

As an online seller, you couldn't ask for a better customer. These Prime Members subscribe at least $99 a year in order to take full advantage of the free shipping that Amazon has to offer.

These Prime Members are not only loyal customers, but they are the ones who tend to purchase items that are more expensive and buy at least %150 more than any of the non-Prime Members. To see these in number basis, they spend around $1,340 on Amazon annually, while non-Prime Members spend only around %529

The use of FBA allows for a wider customer base. There is a speculation of around 50 million Prime Member subscribers in Amazon right now. If you think about, that's a lot of money.

2 - The Care for Shipping, Returns, and Customer Service

Amazon handles everything from picking the item, packing it and shipping it to your customers. Quick and swift shipping gives you happy customers and with happy customers provides with increased sales.

Amazon will also be able to handle any of the unsatisfied customers. This will definitely save the time and money for you because you won't need to employ any additional customer service reps.

Since your items will be stored in Amazon's fulfillment centers, you won't need to gain the headache of where to get the space to fit your inventory.

3 - Buy Box Win

Those in FBA, depending on the category of the product, can place its price at least 10 – 20% higher than the average competitor and still be able to win the Buy Box. That is if you are using FBA and your competitors are not.

This is because shipping is added into the cost. If your items are priced at $20 with a Prime Member shipping, it will beat out a merchant item of $15 with $5 shipping.

4 - Increased Volume of Sales

This may not be a guarantee, but it has been found that those who switch over recognize a rise in unit sales volume to about 20% more. Numerous amounts of sellers have reported higher or even double of their original volume. This is mainly due to the Prime Member subscribers.

5 - Customers are Inclined to Pay More for the Same Product

The millions of Prime Member subscribers on Amazon will know a great deal when they see it. As mentioned in one of the benefits, sellers who are in FBA could factor in the cost of shipping into the price. Some Prime Members are willing to pay a few more bucks to be able to ensure that the delivery is prompted in two days and the added convenience.

6 - No Such Thing as an Inventory Limit

Since Amazon does your inventory for you, you can sell as much as you want without the worry of the amount of storage requirements that you need. Amazon possesses one of the most advanced fulfillment networks in the whole world that will allow you, as a seller, to store as much products as you please with the use of their automated inventory tracker. Your products are guaranteed safety.

YouTube Video Tutorials
- **Amazon FBA: 3 Benefits to Selling on Amazon FBA:** https://goo.gl/LqpiWG
- **Pros and Cons of Selling on Amazon:** https://goo.gl/ecmWV9
- **Amazon FBA Canada: Pros & Cons of FBA** Canada: **https://goo.gl/n5SFra**

f. Disadvantages of Amazon FBA

Like any other business, Amazon FBA also comes with some disadvantages that a seller has to deal with. Here are some Amazon FBA disadvantages you should take in mind:

1 - Not All Products Sold are Profitable with FBA

The products that have a low volume and low margins are the ones that will end up not being profitable to sell with the use of FBA. Furthermore, any items that are heavy and inexpensive low margin items that may require for you to have higher storage fees may be the items that blow out your profits.

2 - Amazon Will Not Be Able to Ship Certain Items

Some items that may be deemed as hazardous are severely prohibited and these items will not be shipped by the Amazon's fulfillment centers. Examples of these items include: any type of flammable liquids, flammable solids, and aerosols. Some beauty products may fall under this category.

3 - Fees, Glorious Fees

FBA may seem like a miracle service, although there are some pitfalls with its use. The biggest one among many of its pitfalls is the numerous amounts of fees associated with FBA.

To start, sellers on Amazon are required to either have a Pro Merchant ($39.95/month) account or the Advantage account ($29.95/year), which have different limitations to what a seller can and cannot do.

Next, FBA charges a certain amount for storage fee for the items that are unsold in Amazon's fulfillment centers. When your items don't sell, FBA customers are charged at rates that can vary from $0.40/cubic foot per month to $0.60 cubic foot per month.

Overall, depending on the type of online business that you are in, you might want to proceed with FBA or not. Take your time to think about it because if it is good for your business it can go far, although if it is not it may destroy what you built.

YouTube Video Tutorials
- Part 1: **What Is FBA? - The Introduction:** https://goo.gl/rJCghN
- Part 2: **Signing up for FBA & Sourcing:** https://goo.gl/dFPMmc
- Part 3: **Organizing and Listing Inventory:** https://goo.gl/VSEpVH
- Part 4: **Rules, Guidelines, and Supplies:** https://goo.gl/QnvW9v
- Part 5: **Packaging Your First Shipment:** https://goo.gl/Wh2uCW, **How to Package Items For Amazon FBA - Save Money & Clear Up Misconceptions:** https://goo.gl/QyZGG6
- Part 6: **Finalizing Your First Shipment:** https://goo.gl/e6ypDK
- All Parts: **The Complete Series:** https://goo.gl/vp8sK2

To get this more advanced book on Amazon FBA, fully packed with highly valuable information, just click the link below to open the Amazon Kindle book page.

Get this book:

View in Amazon Kindle Store: http://goo.gl/6fIafa

Free Resources:

Facebook Page:
www.facebook.com/surefiresuccessnow

Website: www.workathomeentrepreneurblog.com

Made in the USA
Las Vegas, NV
16 January 2024

84379809R00075